The Socialist Challenge Today

The Socialist Challenge Today

SYRIZA, SANDERS, CORBYN

Leo Panitch & Sam Gindin

MERLIN PRESS

Published in 2018 by
The Merlin Press
Central Books Building
Freshwater Road
London
RM8 1RX

www.merlinpress.co.uk

A CIP catalogue record for this book is available from
the British Library

ISBN 978-0-85036-740-9

Printed in the UK by Imprint Digital, Exeter

CONTENTS

Acknowledgements

This little book addresses the challenges facing socialists today by analyzing in historical and theoretical perspective the recent shift from protest to politics on the left. After assessing the expression of this through the Sanders electoral insurgency in the USA, and especially through the Syriza experience in Greece, the book turns to closely examining the limits and possibilities for class, party and state transformation in the context of Jeremy Corbyn's leadership of the Labour Party in Britain.

We wish to thank Tony Zurbrugg of Merlin Press for encouraging us to considerably expand our essay 'Class, party and the challenge of state transformation' in the Socialist Register 2017: *Rethinking Revolution* into this book, as well as thank Adrian Howe for so quickly and expertly preparing it for publication. The analysis offered of both Syriza and the Labour Party owes much to our conversations with too many friends and comrades – a good number themselves political actors as well as observers in Greece and Britain – to mention here. But we especially want to acknowledge the value of our interactions with Max Shanly in relation to following developments in the Labour Party. We dedicate this book to him as well as to his great political mentor, Tony Benn.

Introduction

From social democracy to democratic socialism

In 1917, not only those parties engaged in insurrectionary revolution but even those committed to gradual reform still spoke of eventually transcending capitalism. Half a century later social democrats had explicitly come to define their political goals as compatible with a welfare-state variety of capitalism; and well before the end of the century even many who had formerly embraced the legacy of 1917 would join them in this. Yet this occurred just as the universalization of neoliberalism rendered threadbare any notion of distinct varieties of capitalism. The realism without imagination of the so-called 'Third Way' was shown to lack realism as well as imagination.

However reactionary the era of neoliberal globalization has been, it has seemed to confirm the continuing revolutionary nature of the bourgeoisie, at least in terms of creating 'a world after its own image'.[1] Nevertheless, the financialized form of capitalism that greased the wheels not only of global investment and trade, but also of globally integrated production and consumption, was clearly crisis prone.[2] The first global capitalist crisis of the twenty-first century was rooted in the contradictions attending the new credit-dependent forms through which, amidst stagnant wages in the neoliberal era, mass consumption was sustained. Yet as the crisis has unfolded over the past decade, in sharp contrast to the two great capitalist crises of the twentieth century it did not lead to a replacement of the regime of accumulation that gave rise to it. Unlike the break with the Gold Standard regime in the 1930s and the Bretton Woods regime in the 1970s, neoliberalism persisted. This could be seen in the rescue and reproduction of financial capital, the reassertion of austerity in fiscal policy, the dependence on monetary policy for stimulus, and the further aggravation of income and wealth inequality – all of which was made possible by the continuing economic and political weaknesses of working classes everywhere through this period.

We are now in a new conjuncture. It is a very different conjuncture than the one which led to the perception that neoliberalism, at the height of its embrace by Third Way social democracy, was 'the most successful ideology in world history'.[3] While neoliberal economic practices have been reproduced – as has the American empire's centrality in global capitalism – neoliberalism's legitimacy has been undermined. As the aftershocks of the US financial crash reverberated across the eurozone and the so-called BRICS (Brazil, Russia, India, China, South Africa), this deepened the multiple economic, ecological, and migratory crises that characterize this new conjuncture. At the same time, neoliberalism's ideological delegitimation has enveloped many political institutions that have sustained its practices, from the European Union to political parties at the national level. What makes the current conjuncture so dangerous is the space this has opened for the far right, with its ultra-nationalist, racist, sexist and homophobic overtones, to capture popular frustrations with liberal democratic politics.

The delegitimation of neoliberalism has restored some credibility to the radical socialist case for transcending capitalism as necessary to realize the collective, democratic, egalitarian and ecological aspirations of humanity. It spawned a growing sense that capitalism could no longer continue to be bracketed when protesting the multiple oppressions and ecological threats of our time. And as austerity took top billing over free trade, the spirit of anti-neoliberal protest also shifted. Whereas capitalist globalization had defined the primary focus of oppositional forces in the first decade of the new millennium, the second decade opened with 'Occupy' and the anti-austerity movements in Greece and Spain dramatically highlighting capitalism's gross class inequalities. Yet with this, the insurrectionary flavour of protest without revolutionary effect quickly revealed the limits of forever standing outside the state.

A marked turn on the left from protest to politics has also come to characterize the new conjuncture, as opposition to capitalist globalization shifted from the streets to the state theatres of neoliberal practice. This is in good part what the election of Syriza in Greece and the sudden emergence of *Podemos* in Spain signified. Corbyn's election as leader of the British Labour Party attracted hundreds of thousands of new members with the promise to sustain activism rather than undermine it. And even in the heartland of the global capitalist empire, the short bridge that spanned Occupy and Sanders' left populist promise for a political revolution 'to create a government which represents all Americans and not just the 1%' was reflected in polls indicating that half of all millennials did not support 'capitalism' and held a positive view of 'socialism' – whatever they thought that meant.

This transition from protest to politics has been remarkably class-oriented in terms of addressing inequality in income and wealth distribution, as well as in economic and political power relations. Yet as Andrew Murray has so incisively noted, 'this new politics is generally more class-focused than class-rooted. While it places issues of social inequality and global economic power front and centre, it neither emerges from the organic institutions of the class-in-itself nor advances the socialist perspective of the class-for-itself.'[4] The strategic questions raised by this pertain not only to all the old difficulties of left parties maintaining a class focus once elected; they also pertain to how a class-rooted politics – in the original sense of the connection between working-class formation and political organization – could become transformative today. Given the manifold changes in class composition and identity, as well as the limits and failures of traditional working-class parties and unions in light of these changes, what could this mean in terms of new organizational forms and practices? And what would a class-focused *and* class-rooted transformation of the capitalist state actually entail?

While leaders like Tsipras, Iglesias, Corbyn and Sanders all have pointed beyond Third Way social democracy, their capacity to actually move beyond it is another matter. This partly has to do with their personal limitations, but much more with the specific limitations of each of their political parties, including even the strongest left currents within them, not preparing adequately for the challenge of actually transforming state apparatuses. The experience of the government in Greece highlights this, as well as how difficult it is for governments to extricate their state apparatuses from transnational ones.

All this compels a fundamental rethink of the relationship between class, party and state transformation. If Bolshevik revolutionary discourse seems archaic a hundred years after 1917, it is not just because the legacy of its historic demonstration that revolution was possible has faded. It is also because Gramsci's reframing, so soon after 1917, of the key issues of revolutionary strategy – especially regarding the impossibility of an insurrectionary path to power in states deeply embedded in capitalist societies – rings ever more true. What this means for socialists, however, as we face up to a long war of position in the twenty-first century, is not only the recognition of the limitations of twentieth-century Leninism, let alone Soviet state practices, but also an appreciation of what inspired the communist break with social democracy in the first place. This can be expressed in what Jodi Dean admires today as communism's expression of the 'collective desire for collectivity'; more concretely it encompasses a commitment to working-class internationalism as opposed to national class harmony between capital and labour, an orientation to class formation and organization in the struggle against capital, and a recognition that socialist economic planning requires taking capital away from capital.

Democratic socialism in the twenty-first century must encompass all that was positive about the communist vision even while negating twentieth-century Communist party and state practices by virtue of an indelible commitment to developing democratic capacities to the end of democratizing the economy and the state. This is crucial for retaining a clear distinction between democratic socialism and social democracy. Indeed, given the latter's own history of incorporation into the capitalist state and embrace of neoliberalism, engaging successfully in the long war of position in the twenty-first century will above all require discovering how to avoid the social democratization of those now committed to transcending capitalism. This is the central challenge for socialists today.

1

From class to party

The *Communist Manifesto* of 1848 introduced a new theory of revolution. Against the conspiracies of the few and the experiments of the dreamers, an emerging proletariat was heralded with the potential to usher in a new world. The argument was not that these dispossessed labourers carried revolution in their genes; rather it pointed to their potential for organization, which was facilitated by modern means of communication as well as by the way capitalists collectivized labour. Even though their organization would be 'disrupted time and again by competition amongst the workers themselves', it indeed proved to be the case that 'the ever expanding union of the workers' would lead to 'the organization of workers into a class, and consequently into a political party'.[5]

It was this sense of class formation as process that led E.P. Thompson to argue so powerfully that class was not a static social category but a changing social relationship, which historically took shape in the form of class struggle *before* class. Out of the struggles of the dispossessed labourers against the new capitalist order in England in the last half of the eighteenth century and the first half of the nineteenth came the growing collective identity and community of the working class as a social force.[6] Moreover, as Hobsbawm subsequently emphasized, it was really only in the years from 1870 to 1914 – as proletarianization reached a critical mass, and as workers' organizational presence developed on a national and international scale through mass socialist parties and unions – that the revolutionary potential in the working class that Marx had identified looked set to be realized.[7] However arcane the very term 'workers' state' now may seem, it made sense to people in 1917 – and not least to nervous bourgeoisies.

Yet there was much that made this problematic even then. The fact that so many trade unions had emerged that had nothing to do with socialism reflected how far even the newly organized industrial proletariat stood from revolutionary ambitions. And where there was a commitment to socialist purposes, as was ostensibly the case with the social democratic parties of the Second International, this was compromised in serious ways. The winning of workers' full franchise rights had the contradictory effect of integrating them into the nation state, while the growing separation of leaders from members inside workers' organizations undermined not only accountability, but also the capacity to develop workers' transformative potentials. This was of course contested in these organizations even before Roberto Michels' famous book outlined their oligarchic tendencies.[8] But these two factors – a class-inclusive nationalism and a non-transformative relationship between leaders and led in class organizations – combined to determine why the catastrophic outcome of inter-imperial rivalry announced with the guns of August 1914, far from bringing about the international proletarian revolution, rather ambushed European social democracy into joining the great patriotic war and making truce in the domestic class struggle.

What made proletarian revolution ushering in a workers' state still credible after this – perhaps all the more credible – was the Russian Revolution.

But what Rosa Luxemburg discerned within its first year would definitively mark the outcome: a revolutionary process which in breaking with liberal democracy quickly narrowed rather than broadened the scope of public participation, ending as a 'clique affair'. Lenin, she noted, saw the capitalist state as 'an instrument of oppression of the working class; the socialist state, of the bourgeoisie', but this 'misses the most essential thing: bourgeois class rule has no need of the political training and education of the entire mass of the people, at least not beyond certain narrow limits'. The great danger was that:

Without general elections, without unrestricted freedom of press and assembly, without a free struggle of opinion, life dies out in every public institution, becomes a mere semblance of life, in which only the bureaucracy remains as the active element. Public life gradually falls asleep, a few dozen party leaders of inexhaustible energy and boundless experience direct and rule. Among them, in reality only a dozen outstanding heads do the leading and an elite of the working class is invited from time to time to meetings where they are to applaud the speeches of the leaders, and to approve proposed resolutions unanimously – at bottom then, a clique affair.[9]

20

Isaac Deutscher, looking back some three decades later, succinctly captured the dilemma which had led the Bolsheviks to bring about a dictatorship that would 'at best represent the idea of the class, not the class itself'. He insisted that in consolidating the new regime the Bolsheviks had not 'clung to power for its own sake', but rather that this reflected a deeper quandary. Even though anarcho-syndicalists seemed 'far more popular among the working class', the fact that they 'possessed no positive political programme, no serious organization, national or even local' only reinforced the Bolsheviks identification of the new republic's fate with their own, as 'the only force capable of safeguarding the revolution'.

Lenin's party refused to allow the famished and emotionally unhinged country to vote their party out of power and itself into a bloody chaos. For this strange sequel to their victory the Bolsheviks were mentally quite unprepared. They had always tacitly assumed that the majority of the working class, having backed them in the revolution, would go on to support them unswervingly until they had carried out the full programme of socialism. Naive as the assumption was, it sprang from the notion that socialism was the proletarian idea par excellence and that the proletariat, having once adhered to it, would not abandon it ... It had never occurred to Marxists to reflect whether it was possible or admissible to try to establish socialism regardless of the will of the working class.[10]

The long term effects of what Luxemburg had so quickly understood would contribute to reproducing a dictatorial regime regardless of the will of the working class – and relatedly, also to the gaps in the 'political training and education of the entire mass of the people' – were chillingly captured by what a leader of the local trade union committee at the Volga Automobile Plant said to us in an interview in 1990 just before the regime established in 1917 collapsed: 'Insofar as workers were backward and underdeveloped, this is because there has in fact been no real political education since 1924. The workers were made fools of by the party.'[11] The words here need to be taken literally: the workers were not merely fooled, but *made* into fools; their revolutionary understanding and capacity was undermined.

The fillip that 1917 had given to fuelling workers' revolutionary ambitions worldwide was more than offset by the failure of the revolution in Germany and the Stalinist response to an isolated and beleaguered Soviet Union after

Lenin's death, with all the adverse consequences this entailed. Though the spectre of Bolshevism hardly faded, it was the spectre of fascism that dominated radical change in the interwar years. Nevertheless, there was also widespread recognition of the potential of the working class as the social force most capable of transforming state and society. This perception was not least based on worker organization and class formation during the Great Depression in the USA, which was already by then the new world centre of capitalism. This contributed to the sense on the part of leading American capitalists and state officials as they entered the Second World War that among the barriers to the remaking of a liberal capitalist international order, 'the uprising of [the] international proletariat ... [was] the most significant fact of the last twenty years'.[12]

The strength of the organized working class as it had formed up to the 1950s was registered in the institutionalization of collective bargaining and welfare reforms. The effects of this were highly contradictory. The material gains in terms of individual and family consumption, which workers obtained directly or indirectly from collective bargaining for rising wages as well as from a social wage largely designed to secure and

23

supplement that consumption, were purchased at the cost of union and party practices that attenuated working-class identity and community – especially in light of the restructuring of employment, residency and education that accompanied these developments. To be sure, the continuing salience of working-class organization was palpable. This was increasingly so in the public sector, but it was also measurable in class struggles in the private sector which resisted workplace restructuring, as well as in the wage-led inflation that contributed to the capitalist profitability crisis of the 1970s. Yet the failure to renew and extend working-class identity and community through these struggles opened the way to the neoliberal resolution of the crises of the 1970s through a widespread assault on trade unionism and the welfare state, and the interpellation of workers themselves as 'taxpayers'.

By the beginning of the twenty-first century, aided by the realization of a fully global capitalism and the networked structures of production, finance and consumption that constitute it, there were more workers on the face of the earth than ever before. New technologies certainly restricted job growth in certain sectors, but this was accompanied by entirely new sectors in both manufacturing and especially high tech services. Though this weakened the leverage of class struggles in important ways, it also introduced new points of strategic potential: strikes at component plants or interruptions of supplier chains at warehouses and ports could force shutdowns throughout a globally integrated production network, and whistleblowing could expose vast stores of information hidden by corporations and states.

The precarious conditions workers increasingly face today, even when they belong to unions, speaks not to a new class division between pre-cariat and proletariat. Precariousness rather reflects how previous processes of working-class formation and organization have become undone. Precariousness is not something new in capitalism: employers have always tried to gain access to labour when they want, dispose of it as they want and, in between, use it with as few restrictions as possible. There is in this context limited value in drawing new sociological nets of who is or is not in the working class. Rather than categorizing workers into different strata – nurses or baristas, teachers or software developers, farmhands or truckers, salespeople or bank-tellers

– what needs to preoccupy our imaginations and inform our strategic calculations is how to visualize and how to develop the potential of new forms of working-class organization and formation in the twenty-first century.

There are indeed multitudes of workers' struggles taking place today in the face of an increasingly exploitative and chaotic capitalism. Yet there is no denying that prospects for working-class transformative agency seem dim. Factors internal to working-class institutions, their contradictions and weaknesses, allowed – in the developing as well as the developed countries – for the passage of free trade, the liberalization of finance, the persistence of austerity, the further commodification of labour power, the restructuring of all dimensions of economic and social life in today's global capitalism. The inability of the working class to renew itself and discover new organizational forms in light of the dynamism of capital and capacities of the state to contain worker resistance has allowed the far right today to articulate and contextualize a set of common sentiments linked to the crisis – frustrations with insecurity and inequality and anger with parties that once claimed to represent workers' interests. Escaping this crisis of the working class is not primarily a matter of better policies or better tactics. It is primarily an *organizational* challenge to facilitate new processes of class formation rooted in the multiple dimensions of workers' lives that encompass so many identities and communities.

2

Signposts towards democratic socialism

Developing socialist parties of a new kind will be required to overcome the crisis of the working class. It was the exhaustion of both Social Democratic and Communist parties as agents of social transformation that in good part fuelled the radicalism of the New Left in the 1960s. Although the student radicalism and industrial militancy of the late 1960s led to a sharp turn by activists to extra-parliamentary forms of activity, the reverberations were bound to be felt in the parties as well. This entailed, first of all, a revival of a democratic socialist discourse in party debates. In particular, the language of 'class', of 'movement', of 'capital', of 'exploitation', of 'crisis', of 'struggle', of 'imperialism', even of 'transformation', while never entirely extirpated from Social Democratic parties, had certainly become marginalized within them in the decades after the Second World War. By the early 1970s, all this was again within constant earshot at party meetings and conferences. Even the term `social democracy' was often used pejoratively, and one suddenly found even many of the most jaded leaders now calling themselves `democratic socialists'.

But more than language was involved: there was a programmatic turn as well, in which the questions of taking capital away from capital through major extensions of public or workers' ownership (or at least through radical measures of investment planning and industrial democracy) and the pursuit of a foreign policy independent of the United States, came onto the agendas of some of these parties. Certainly only the most naive observer or participant could have thought in the 1970s that these parties had actually been transformed into effective vehicles for a socialist transition; the more cynical remained convinced that these parties were in the process of recon- structing their viability as mediating agencies for the consensual reproduction of capitalism and the containment of industrial militancy and radical structural reform. Nonetheless, the new discourse and programmatic thrust did carry with it an explicit critique of established social democratic practice.

The question remained, of course, of whether socialism could be placed back on the agenda, not only of these parties, but in the broader political arena. It certainly cannot be claimed that there was a ready-made groundswell of socialist electoral opinion just waiting to be tapped: it needed to be created in the interplay between party discourse and popular experience. The eventual victories in the early 1980s of the French, Greek and Swedish parties on the basis of the most radical programmes put before their electorates at least since the 1940s certainly invalidated simplistic claims that parties which advanced such a programme were inherently unelectable. Yet if a socialist alternative was to not only avoid conjuring up a negative electoral reaction, but to produce the popular support needed to sustain a socialist government's radical thrust, this depended on a sea-change in the organizational and ideological practices of parliamentary social-ist parties themselves. They had to become un-ified around the socialist alternative; they had to find the means to be effective vehicles for a transformation and mobilization of popular attitudes; they had to develop mechanisms to ensure that their leaderships not only mouthed a socialist discourse that the activists wanted to hear at party meetings, but shared a commitment to radical change and maintained such a commitment even once subject to the conservatizing pressures of office.

It was a tall order indeed. The programmatic changes that occurred in a number of social democratic parties in the 1970s were obviously developed with some awareness of these questions: as in the emphasis placed on industrial democracy alongside nationalization and investment controls, or on the decentralized socialization of capital through trade-union and community-administered wage-earners' funds. These policies were conceived with a view to popularizing a socialist alternative via obviating its association with the authoritarian practices of Eastern European 'actually existing socialisms' as well as the bureaucratic practices of state-owned enterprises in the West. But this was itself a small first step. For even to make this credible and popular, fundamental organizational changes within the social democratic parties themselves were necessary to make them effective vehicles for a democratic socialist alternative.

32

In every case the established forces in these parties succeeded in seeing off the challenge this represented. In some case this happened quickly, as with the expulsion in the early 1970s of the Young Socialists in the German SPD and the Movement for an Independent Socialist Canada in the New Democratic Party; in other cases, it took over a decade, as in Sweden with the watering down of the wage-earners funds project for socializing capital, or in France with the U-turn of the Mitterand government in the early 1980s. The most promising and most protracted intra-party struggle occurred in the British Labour Party around the Alternative Economic Strategy and the Campaign for Labour Party Democracy running through the 1970s until the defeat of the Bennite insurgency in the early 1980s, aided by a coalition of old left parliamentarians and union leaders.[13]

These intra-party struggles, including those between the Eurocommunists and the old guard in the Communist parties, fuelled a much broader discussion on the European left, represented by Gorz, Magri, Benn, Miliband, Poulantzas, Rowbotham, Segal and Wainwright among others, oriented to discovering new strategic directions. They pointed beyond both the Leninist and

Social Democratic 'models' which, despite taking different routes, nevertheless evinced in their practices a common distrust of popular capacities to democratize state structures.[14]

This was especially well articulated in Poulantzas's, 'Towards a Democratic Socialism'.[15] 'There is no longer a question of building "models" of any kind whatsoever. All that is involved is a set of signposts which, drawing lessons of the past, point out the traps to anyone wishing to avoid certain well-known destinations', not least the 'techno-bureaucratic statism of the experts'. This was the outcome not only of the instrumentalist strategic conception of social democratic parliamentarism, but also of the 'Leninist dual-power type of strategy which envisages straightforward replacement of the state apparatus with an apparatus of councils'. In both cases, '[t]ransformation of the state apparatus does not really enter into the matter':

> first of all the existing state power is taken and then another is put in its place. This view of things can no longer be accepted. If taking power denotes a shift in the relationship of forces within the state, and if it is recognized that this will involve a long process of change, then the seizure of state power will entail

concomitant transformations of its apparatuses ... In abandoning the dual-power strategy, we do not throw overboard, but pose in a different fashion, the question of the state's materiality as a specific apparatus.

Notably, Poulantzas went back to Luxemburg's critique of Lenin in 1918 to stress the importance of socialists building on liberal democracy, even while transcending it, in order to provide the space for mass struggles to unfold which could 'modify the relationship of forces within the state apparatuses, themselves the strategic site of political struggle'. The very notion *to take* state power 'clearly lacks the strategic vision of a process of transition to socialism – that is of a long stage during which the masses will act to conquer power and transform state apparatuses'. For the working class to displace the old ruling class, in other words, it must develop capacities to democratize the state, which must always rest on 'increased intervention of the popular masses in the state ... certainly through their trade union and political forms of representation, but also through their own initiatives within the state itself'. To expect that institutions of direct democracy outside the state can simply displace the old state in a single revolutionary rupture in fact avoided all the difficult questions of political representation in the transition to and under socialism.

Indeed, as André Gorz had already insisted in his pathbreaking essay on 'Reform and Revolution' a decade earlier, taking off from liberal democracy on 'the peaceful road to socialism' was not a matter of adopting 'an *a priori* option for gradualism; nor of an *a priori* refusal of violent revolution or armed insurrection. It is a consequence of the latter's actual impossibility in the European context.'[16] The advancement of what Gorz called a 'socialist strategy of progressive reforms' did not mean the 'installation of islands of socialism in a capitalist ocean', but rather involved the types of 'structural reforms' or 'non-reformist reforms' which could not be institutionalized so as to close off class antagonism but which allowed for further challenges to the balance of power and logic of capitalism, and thereby introduce a dynamic that allowed the process to go further. In calling for the creation of new 'centres of social control and direct democracy' outside the state, Gorz was far-sighted in terms of what this could contribute to a broad process of new class formation with transformative potential, not least by extending to 'the labour of ideological research' and more generally to the transformative capacities of 'cultural labour aiming at the overthrow of norms and schemata of social consciousness'. This would be essential for ensuring that 'the revolutionary movements' capacity for action and hegemony is enriched and confirmed by its capacity to inspire ... the autonomous activity of town planners, architects, doctors, teachers and psychologists'.[17]

What this left aside, however, were the crucial changes in state structures that would need to attend this process. Poulantzas went to the heart of the matter, a decade later, stressing that on 'the democratic road to socialism, the long process of taking power essentially consists in the spreading, development, coordination and direction of those diffuse centres of resistance which the masses always possess within the state networks, in such a way that they become real centres of power on the strategic terrain of the state'. Even Gramsci, as Poulantzas pointed out, 'was unable to pose the problem in all its amplitude' since his 'war of position' was conceived as the application of Lenin's model/strategy to the 'different concrete conditions of the West' without actually addressing how to change state apparatuses.[18]

Yet it must also be said that Poulantzas, even while highlighting the need for taking up the challenge of state transformation, did not himself get very far in detailing what actually changing the materiality of state apparatuses would entail in specific instances. Lurking here was the theoretical problem Miliband had identified of not differentiating state power from class power, and therefore not specifying sufficiently how the modalities and capacities involved in exercising capitalist state power would be changed into different modalities with structurally transformative capacities.[19] And as Goran Therborn pointed out, in envisaging an important role for unions of state employees in the process of transforming state apparatuses, it was necessary to address the problem that 'state bureaucrats and managers will not thereby disappear, and problems of popular control will remain', thereby continuing to pose 'serious and complicated questions' for the state transformation through socialist democracy.[20]

Socialists have since paid far too little attention to the challenges this poses.[21] While the recognition that neither insurrectionary politics to 'smash the state' nor the social democratic illusion of using the extant state to introduce progressive policies became more and more widespread, this was accompanied with a penchant for developing 'market socialist' models in the late 1980s. And this has subsequently been succeeded by a spate of radical left literature that – in almost a mirror image of neoliberalism's championing of private corporations and small business firms against the state – weakly points to examples of cooperatives and self-managed enterprises as directly bearing socialist potential.[22] Replicated here is exactly what Poulantzas identified in the conception of those for whom 'the only way to avoid statism is to place oneself outside the state. The way forward would then be, without going as far as dual power simply to block the path of the state from the outside.' Yet by concentrating exclusively on 'breaking power up and scattering it among an infinity of micro-powers', the result is that the 'movement is prevented from intervening in actual transformations of the state, and the two processes are simply kept running along parallel lines'.[23]

3

Sanders and Syriza:
from protest to politics

'Election days come and go. But political and social revolutions that attempt to transform our society never end.' The speech with which Bernie Sanders closed his Democratic primary election campaign began with these sentences; it ended by expressing the hope that future historians would trace all the way back to the 'political revolution' of 2016 'how our country moved forward into reversing the drift toward oligarchy, and created a government which represents all the people and not just the few'.[24] It is tempting to treat as ersatz the rhetoric of revolution deployed here, taking the meaning of the word from the sublime to the ridiculous, or from tragedy to farce. The last time an American politician vying for the presidency issued a call for a political revolution it came from

Ronald Reagan. But for all the limits of Sanders' populist campaign, the national attention and massive support garnered by a self-styled democratic socialist who positively associated the term revolution with the struggle against class inequality in fact represented a major discursive departure in American political life, which can be a resource for further socialist organizing.

Of course, the specific policy measures advanced by Sanders were, as he constantly insisted, reforms that had at some point been introduced in other capitalist societies. But when the call for public medicare for all, or free college tuition, or infrastructure renewal through direct public employment, is explicitly attached to a critique of a ruling class which wields corporate and financial power through the direct control of parties, elections and the media, this goes beyond the bounds of what can properly be dismissed as mere reformism, even if the demands hardly evoke what the call for bread, land and peace did in 1917. And it is no less a significant departure, especially in the US, to make class inequality the central theme of a political campaign in a manner designed to span and penetrate race and gender divisions to the end of building a more coherent class force. By explicitly posing the question of who stands to benefit more from high quality public health care and education and well compensated work opportunities than African-Americans and Latinos, Sanders highlighted the need to move beyond the ghettoes of identity.

The key question is whether Sanders' campaign really could lay the grounds for an ongoing political movement capable of effecting this 'political revolution'. Sanders' argument during the campaign that he could be sustained in the White House amidst a hostile Congress and imperial state apparatus by a 'mass movement' marching on Washington D.C. was not very convincing. Much more serious was his call after he lost the primary campaign for a shift from protest to politics at every level, including 'school boards, city councils, county commissions, state legislatures and governorships'.

The very fact that the Sanders campaign was class-focused rather than class-rooted may be an advantage here. It opens space for a new politics that can become 'rooted' in the sense of being grounded in working-class struggles but committed to the radical transformation of the generally exhausted institutions of the labour movement. This ranges across turning union branches into centres of working-class life, leading the fight for collective public services, breaking down the oligarchic relationship between leaders and led, contributing to building the broadest member capacities, emphasizing the importance of expressing a clearer class sensibility, and even becoming ambitious enough to introduce socialist ideas. This also applies to Workers Action Centers, which have spread across the US but which are so often overwhelmed by having to reproduce themselves financially in order to continue providing vital services to Black, Latino, immigrant and women workers. Becoming more class-rooted and effective would require building the institutional capacities to creatively organize workers in different sectors into new city-wide organizations, as well as develop a coordinating national infrastructure.

Similar challenges would need to be put to consumer and credit co-operatives, which are broadly identified with the left, but whose primarily narrow economic activities need to be politicized, above all in the sense of opening their spaces to radical education about the capitalist context in which they operate, actively participating in left campaigns, and contributing a portion of their revenue to funding organizers to carry out such tasks. And to get beyond the frustrations so often voiced in the environmental movement with workers' defensive prioritization of their jobs, turning this into a positive rather than negative class focus by speaking in terms of 'just transitions' to a clean energy economy would also mean raising the necessity for economic planning to address both environmental and social crises, with the corollary of challenging the prerogatives of private property and capitalist power structures.

A new class politics cannot emerge *ex nihilo*, however. The Sanders campaign, initiated by an outsider in the Democratic Party, confirmed that if you are not heard in the media you are not broadly heard. Yet whatever the advantages of initially mobilizing from within established institutions in this respect, the impossibility of a political revolution taking place under the auspices of the Democratic Party needs to be directly faced. After it had become clear he would not clinch the nomination, Sanders and the movement that had begun to take shape around him appeared at risk of falling into a myopic strategy of internally transforming and democratizing the Democratic Party. In part, this is one of the contradictions in Sanders' choice to run as a Democrat. While the Sanders campaign showed that Democratic Party institutions offer certain bases from which to advance a left politics – lending his campaign a certain legitimacy and credibility within mainstream discourse – in the long run, an alternative political pole will have to be constructed around which social struggles can condense.

It was far from surprising that the thousands of Sanders supporters who gathered at the People's Summit in Chicago after the primary campaign ended did not come there to found a new party. What happened there, as Dan La Botz described it, 'was about vision, not organization or strategy', so that one could at best only hear 'the sound made by the *Zeitgeist* passing though the meeting rooms and the halls, brushing up against us, making its way, sometimes gracefully, sometimes clumsily, to the future'.[25] One key test will be whether, as it 'makes its way', lessons are learned from the US Labor Party project of the 1990s, and links are made with attempts already underway to spawn new socialist political formations, escaping the traces of either Bolshevik sectarianism or 'Third World' romanticism as well as the naïve admiration for Canadian and European social democracy that has long characterized so much of the US left.[26]

This takes us from Sanders to Syriza, the only party to the left of traditional social democracy in Europe that has actually succeeded in winning a national election since the current economic crisis began. Syriza's roots go back to the formation of Synaspismos, first as an electoral alliance in the 1980s, and then as an independent, although factionalized, new party in the early 1990s. This was part of the broader institutional reconfiguration inaugurated by the Eurocommunist strategic orientation, searching for a way forward in the face of Communist as well as Social Democratic parties having lost their historic roles and capacities as agencies of working-class political representation and social transformation. This search went all the way back to the 1960s and accelerated after the collapse of the Soviet bloc and social democracy's embrace of the 'Third Way'. In Greece especially, the Eurocommunist orientation was characterized by continuing to embrace the tradition of political revolution as experienced in the Civil War after 1945, even while distancing itself from the Soviet regime; and it would increasingly be characterized by the inspiration it took from, and a willingness to work with, new social movements.

Synaspismos through the 1990s offered enthusiastic support for European integration, but as the neoliberal form of Economic and Monetary Union buried the promises of a European Social Charter, the grounds were laid in Greece, as elsewhere on the European radical left, for a more 'Eurosceptical' orientation.[27] This new critical posture towards the European variety of capitalism was a crucial element in Synaspismos explicitly defining, by the turn of the millennium, its strategic goal as 'the socialist transformation of Greek society' while increasingly encouraging 'dialogue and common actions' not only with the alter-globalization movement, but with radical ecologists and political groups of a Trotskyist or Maoist lineage. The goal of the Coalition of the Radical Left, with the acronym Syriza, which emerged out of this as an electoral alliance was designed, as Michalis Spourdalakis put it, 'not so much to unify but rather to connect in a flexible fashion the diverse actions, initiatives and movements ... and to concern itself with developing popular political capacities as much as with changing state policy'. But actually turning Synaspismos, and through it Syriza, into such a party was, as Spourdalakis immediately adds, 'more wishful thinking than realistic prospect'.[28]

As the eurocrisis broke, however, with Greece

at the epicentre of the attempt to save the euro through the application of severe austerity at its weakest point, all the elements of Syriza threw themselves into the 2011 wave of protests, occupations and strikes, while supporting the 400 or so community solidarity networks around the country to help the worst affected cope. This prepared the ground for Syriza's electoral breakthrough of 2012. Syriza's active insertion into the massive outbursts of social protest from below across Greece the year before was a source of radical democratic energy that went far beyond what can be generated during an election campaign, however successful. What this meant was eloquently articulated at Syriza's Congress in 2013 when it finally turned itself from an electoral alliance into a single party political organization.

The conclusion to Syriza's refounding political resolution called for 'something more' than the programmatic framework that resolution set out. Since 'for a Government of the Left, a parliamentary majority – whatever its size – is not enough', the something more it called for was 'the creation and expression of the widest possible, militant and catalytic political movement of multidimensional subversion'.

Only such a movement can lead to a Government of the Left and only such a movement can safeguard the course of such a government ... [which] carries out radical reforms, takes on development initiatives and other initiatives of a clear environmental and class orientation, opens up new potentials and opportunities for popular intervention, helps the creation of new forms of popular expression and claims ... Syriza has shouldered the responsibility to contribute decisively to the shaping of this great movement of democratic subversion that will lead the country to a new popular, democratic, and radical changeover.[29]

This sort of language, articulating this sort of understanding, was rare on the European radical left, let alone anywhere else. Yet as the Syriza leadership contemplated the dilemmas it faced as it stood on the doorstep of government, its concern to appear as a viable government in the media's eyes led them to concentrate, as was evident in the Thessalonika Manifesto proclaimed just a year later, on refining and scaling down the policy proposals in the 2013 party programme. This was done with little internal party consultation. Moreover, the leadership was mainly concerned with finding enough experienced and efficient personnel to bring into the state to change the notoriously clientelistic and corrupt state apparatus. Little attention was paid to who would be left in the party to act as an organizing cadre in society.

Notably the increase in party membership was not at all proportionate to the extent of the electoral breakthrough. Even when new radical activists did join, the leadership generally did very little to support those in the party apparatus who wanted to develop these activists' capacities to turn party branches into centres of working-class life and strategically engage with them, preferably in conjunction with the Solidarity Networks, in planning for alternative forms of production and consumption. All this spoke to how far Syriza still was from having discovered how to escape the limits of social democracy.

4

Syriza and the problem of state transformation

[This] is not a 'betrayal'. It's not about the well-known scenario 'they have sold out'. We have seen that there was real confrontation. We have seen the amount of pressure, the blackmailing by the European Central Bank. We have seen that they want to bring the Syriza government to its knees. And they need to do that because it represents a real threat, not some kind of illusion of a reformist type. So the reality is that the representatives of the Greek government did the best they could. But they did it within the wrong framework and with the wrong strategy and, in this sense, the outcome couldn't have been different ... The people who think that 'the reformists will fail' and that somehow in the wings stands the revolutionary vanguard who is waiting to take over somehow and lead the masses to a victory are I think completely outside of reality.[30]

All this was said within a month of Syriza's election at the end of January 2015 by Stathis Kouvelakis, whose interpretation of the dramatic unfolding of events in his country garnered widespread attention on the international left. Himself a member's of Syriza's Central Committee as a partisan of the Left Platform, he was speaking at a meeting in London and addressing the disappointments already felt when the new government agreed to renew negotiations with the EU and IMF. Less than five months later, as these negotiations infamously came to a climax, he would, along with many others, leave Syriza in response to what he now called the government's 'capitulation', which indeed became the most common epithet used by the international left. Yet the need to ask whether the outcome could really have been different was now greater than ever. And while the answer did indeed hinge on the adequacy of Syriza's strategy in relation to Europe, that in turn related to deeper issues of party organization, capacity building and state transformation – as well as the adequacy of strategies on the wider European left, at least in terms of shifting the overall balance of forces.

The common criticism of Syriza, strongly advanced by the Left Platform, was that it had not developed a 'Plan B' for leaving the eurozone and adopting an alternate currency as the key condition for rejecting neoliberal austerity and cancelling debt obligations. What this criticism recoiled from admitting was that the capital and import controls this also would require would lead to Greece being forced out of the EU as a whole. After 35 years of integration, the institutional carapace for capitalism in Greece was provided by the many ways the state apparatus became entangled with the EU. Breaking out of this would have required Syriza as a party and government to be prepared for an immediate systemic rupture. It could certainly be said that Syriza was naïve to believe that it could stop the European economic torture while remaining in the eurozone, let alone the EU. At the very least, this simultaneously posed two great challenges: could the Greek state be fundamentally changed while remaining within the EU, and could the EU itself be fundamentally changed from within at the initiative of that state?

For a small country without significant oil resources, a break with the EU would have entailed economic isolation (along the lines of that endured by the Cuban revolution, yet without the prospect of anything like its geostrategic and economic support from the former USSR). The Syriza government faced the intractable contradiction that to fulfil its promise to stop the EU's economic torture, it would have to leave the EU – which would, given the global as well as European balance of forces and the lack of alternative production and consumption capabilities in place, lead to further economic suffering for an unforeseeable period. Despite the massive popular mobilization the government unleashed by calling the referendum in July to support its position against that of the EU-IMF, the dilemma was the same as it had been when it first entered the state. That the government managed to win re-election in the fall of the 2015 while succumbing to and implementing the diktats of the 'Institutions' indicated that Kouvelakis's observation when it entered into the negotiations back in February still held: 'People support the government because the perception they have is that they couldn't act otherwise in that very specific situation. They really see that the balance of forces was extremely uneven.'

Costas Douzinas, another prominent London-based Greek intellectual newly elected as a Syriza member of parliament in the fall of 2015, outlined the 'three different temporalities' through which the radical left must 'simultaneously live' once it enters the state.[31] There is 'the time of the present': the dense and difficult time when the Syriza government – 'held hostage' to the creditors as a 'quasi-protectorate' of the EU and IMF – is required 'to implement what they fought against', and thus 'to legislate and apply the recessional and socially unjust measures it ideologically rejects'. This raises 'grave existential issues and problems of conscience' which cannot go away, but can be 'soothed through the activation of two other temporalities that exist as traces of futurity in the present time'.

This begins with 'the medium term of three to five years', when time for the government appears 'slower and longer' as it probes for the space it needs to implement its 'parallel program' so as not only to 'mitigate the effects of the memorandum' but also to advance 'policies with a clear left direction … in close contact with the party and the social movements'. This is the bridge to the third and longest temporality, 'the time of the radical left vision', which will be reached 'only by continuously and simultaneously implementing and undermining the agreement policies'. As this third temporality starts unfolding, freed from the neoliberal lambast, 'the full programme of the left of the 21st century' will emerge. 'It is a case of escaping into the future, acting now from the perspective of a future perfect, of what will have been. In this sense, the future becomes an active factor of our present.'

This scenario was only plausible insofar as what distinguished Syriza from social democratic governments in the neoliberal era, even as it implemented the neoliberal measures forced upon it, was its refusal to embrace neoliberal ideology. The really crucial condition for the three temporalities to coexist, however, is precisely the 'close contact with the party and the social movements', which Douzinas only mentions in passing. Even in terms of its relations to the party, let alone the social movements, the Syriza government failed to escape from familiar social democratic patterns as it distanced itself from party pressures. It seemed incapable of appreciating the need for activating party cadre to develop social capacities to lay the grounds for temporality two and eventually three.

The neglect of the party had already turned to offhand dismissal when the government called the second election of 2015. As so many of its leading cadre left the party in the face of this – including even the General Secretary, who also resigned rather than asserting the party's independence from the government – the promise that Syriza might escape the fate of social democracy in neoliberal capitalism was left in tatters. There are still those in Syriza, inside and outside the government, who, operating with something very like the three temporalities in mind, are trying to revive the party outside government as the key agent of transformation. But whether they can manage to create the conditions for 'Syriza to be Syriza again' is now moot indeed.[32]

Yet the problem goes far deeper. It was ironically those who advanced the ostensibly more radical Plan B who seemed to treat state power most instrumentally. Little or no attention was paid by them on how to disentangle a very broad range of state apparatuses from budgetary dependence on EU funding, let alone to the transformations the Greek state apparatuses would have to undergo merely to administer the controls and rationing required to manage the black and grey markets that would have expanded inside and outside the state if Greece exited the eurozone. This was especially problematic given the notorious clientelistic and corrupt state practices which Syriza as a party had been vociferously committed to ending, but once in government did not have the time to change, even where the inclination to do so was still there. When confronted with a question on how to deal with this, one leading advocate of Plan B responded privately that in such a moment of rupture it is necessary to shoot people. But this only raised the bigger question of whom the notoriously reactionary coercive apparatuses of the Greek state, as unchanged as they were, would be most likely to listen to, and most likely to shoot.

Perhaps most tellingly, advocates of Plan B showed no more, and often rather less, interest in democratizing state apparatuses by linking them with social movements. This stood in contrast with the minister of social services, who had herself been the key founder of the federation of solidarity networks, Solidarity4All.[33] She openly spoke to her frustrations that Syriza MPs, even while paying over a sizeable portion of their salaries to the networks, insisted that they alone should be the conduits for contact with solidarity activists in their communities.

The Minister of Education visited one school a week and did tell teachers, parents and students that if they wanted to use the school as a base for changing social relations in their communities they would have his support. However, the

Ministry of Education itself did not become actively engaged in promoting the use of schools as community hubs, neither providing spaces for activists organizing around food and health services, nor the technical education appropriate to this, nor other special programmes to prepare students to spend periods of time in communities, contributing to adult education and working on community projects.

Yet it must be said that the social movements themselves were largely passive and immobilized in this respect, as if waiting for the government to deliver. Activists from the networks of food solidarity were rightly frustrated earlier that they could not get from the Minister of Agriculture the information they asked for on the locations of specific crops so they might approach a broader range of farmers. But they did not see it as their responsibility to develop and advance proposals on how the agriculture ministry could have been changed under the Syriza government so as to do this; or more ambitiously so as identify idle land to be given over to community food production co-ops, and in coordinating this across sub-regions; or even more ambitiously, how the defence ministry might have been changed so that military trucks (at least those sitting idle between demonstrations) could be used to facilitate the distribution of food through the solidarity networks.

Insofar as the Syriza government has failed the most crucial democratic, let alone revolutionary test, of linking the administration up with popular forces – not just for meeting basic needs but also for planning and implementing the restructuring of economic and social life – there were all too few on the radical left outside the state who really saw this as a priority either. The charges of capitulation and betrayal that emanated from an understandably disappointed radical left inside and outside Greece should have been tempered in light of this. There was a marked lack of seriousness, if not dishonesty, behind the tendency to treat the referendum as proving, not just the massive public support for resisting further Troika-imposed draconian austerity (which was the question actually posed) but that the same support would have existed for leaving the eurozone, and most likely the EU, in light of the capital and import controls that this inevitably would have led to.

To say this is not to have any illusions about the EU itself, or about what the Syriza government ended up doing in accommodating to it. Insofar as the majority of Greeks still did want to remain in the EU, Syriza's critics from the left failed to politically acknowledge what the people themselves practically understood, which was precisely the further costs that this would have entailed in terms of adding to their suffering insofar as Greece would have been left economically isolated, or even subject to a military coup or civil war. Syriza did not create the conditions in which people were prepared to risk this. But there is no point in wishing those conditions into existence. The challenge for democratic socialists is to confront this and work towards creating them.

5

Corbyn's challenge: from insurgency to transformation?

The enormous enthusiasm generated by the campaign to elect Jeremy Corbyn to the leadership of the British Labour Party in the summer of 2015 signalled – amidst the delegitimation of neoliberal globalization – the staying power of the shift from protest to politics on the left. This confounded expectations that the disappointment of the high hopes invested in the Syriza government at the beginning of that year would have debilitating effects across the international left. And if it was surprising enough that Corbyn should have been elected as party leader, even more surprising was how far this came to be electorally validated two years later in June 2017, through Corbyn leading the party to the largest increase in its vote in any general election since 1945.

The Corbyn phenomenon raises all the old questions associated with the limits and possibilities of democratizing and radicalizing those old working-class parties through which social struggles from below had come to be channelled into the narrow framework of actually-existing capitalist democracies. It is important to recall Ralph Miliband's sobering judgement in the 1976 *Socialist Register* that 'the belief in the effective transformation of the Labour Party into an instrument of socialist policies is the most crippling of all illusions to which socialists in Britain have been prone'. Yet it is no less important to recall his observations on the inability of the socialist left in Britain to create any effective 'organization of its own political formation, able to attract a substantial measure of support'.[34] In the continuing absence of anything like Syriza's sprouting from the intertwining roots of Eurocommunism and new social movements in Greece, it perhaps should not have been quite so surprising that as the crisis of neoliberalism brought New Labour down after 2008, the prospect of transforming the Labour Party would once again emerge as a plausible strategic option for the British left.

The sudden reinvestment of considerable socialist hope, energy and creativity in the Labour Party under Jeremy Corbyn's leadership was epitomized by the filmmaker Ken Loach, who in 2013 had stood at the forefront of yet another futile attempt to launch a serious socialist electoral alternative (Left Unity).[35] By 2017 Loach could be found making campaign videos for the Labour Party featuring a very broad range of working people demanding 'the full fruits of our labour'. To be sure, even under Corbyn, it was still almost unimaginable that the Labour Party, absent Greece's legacy of a revolutionary communist political culture, would echo Syriza's rhetoric in calling for 'the creation and expression of the widest possible, militant and catalytic political movement of multidimensional subversion'. On the other hand, for all the attempts by New Labour to distance itself from the party's class roots, these remained far more deeply embedded in working-class communities and the trade unions than was the case with Syriza. What fuelled popular support for all the recent party insurgencies was a common reaction to neoliberal austerity and the complicity of centre-left politicians in it. Yet those who fomented the Corbyn insurgency were far more conscious, based on decades of experience, that making the shift from protest to politics really effective would entail a profound transformation in party structures.

The explosion of 1960s activism marked Corbyn's early political development. Although the fact that almost the last place most of these new activists were initially attracted to was the Labour party already points to one of the most important differences between the earlier attempt to transform the party in the 1970s, spearheaded by Corbyn's mentor Tony Benn, and the one spearheaded by Corbyn himself so many decades later, which became the catalyst for drawing hundreds of thousands new members to the party.

Corbyn's own political formation took place as part of the last serious attempt to effect a radical democratic socialist transformation of the Labour Party amidst the terminal crisis of the postwar Keynesian welfare state in the 1970s. Although this had already been defeated by the time Corbyn was first elected as an MP in 1983, Corbyn was attracted by Tony Benn's vision to counter the basically undemocratic market alternative to social democracy 'now emerging everywhere on the right' by connecting the Labour Party to the political energy fuelling the student uprisings, worker militancy and radical community politics. Benn's message that 'our long campaign to democratise power in Britain has, first, to begin in our own movement' above all involved extending 'our representative function so as to bring ourselves into a more creative relationship with many organizations that stand outside our membership'. The promise of Benn's appeal was thus that 'a Labour government will never rule again but will try to create the conditions under which it is able to act as the natural partner of a people, who really mean something more than we thought they did, when they ask for self-government'.[36]

The strategic orientation of the Campaign for Labour Party Democracy (CLPD) to initially concentrate the democratic impulse inward produced intense opposition from the establishment forces in the party, who projected the decade-long intra-party struggle outward as an assault on the integrity of the British state. This blunted the processes of democratic socialist persuasion, education and mobilization not only so necessary for short-term electoral success but, in a longer term perspective, for the party to become an active agent of new working-class formation and capacity development. The defeat of democratic forces inside the party, well before the 1983 election, eventually led to the New Labour project of not only accommodating to Thatcherism but also stifling any trace of socialist sentiment as well as intra-party democracy.

As Alex Nunns has shown, the emergence in the early 2000s of a new generation of union leaders began to lay the foundations for a fundamental break with New Labour: 'From being the Praetorian guard of the leadership they became the internal opposition ... [and] embarked on a structural battle with the Blairite machine.' This in turn once again highlighted the importance of the old Campaign for Labour Party Democracy and its capacity for 'navigating the party structures'.[37] It also gave new life to the small coterie of MPs in the Socialist Campaign Group of the PLP (among them, John MacDonnell and Diane Abbot stood before Corbyn in the earlier leadership elections, and Jon Trickett had originally been expected to stand in 2015). One of the most important foundations for the Corbyn insurgency was laid almost a decade before when Michael Meacher, a close ally of Benn's ever since he was elected as a young MP in 1970, took on as his parliamentary assistant one of the CLPD's original young stalwarts, Jon Lansman. He was directed to stay away from Westminster and instead work full time to revive and deepen the alliance with left-wing constituency and trade union activists.

It was the ability of the new generation of union leaders to secure their members' votes for Ed Miliband, on the basis of his disavowal of New Labour, which got him elected as leader in 2010. Yet as Richard Seymour observed: 'It was an integral part of Ed Miliband's strategy for reviving and rebranding Labour that it should seek a new synthesis of left and right.' His accommodation to the Blairites who still dominated the Parliamentary Labour Party (PLP) countered 'pressure from trade unionists and constituency activists to move further to the left than he wished to go'.[38] Keeping his distance from Socialist Campaign Group MPs as well as the new union leaders (who his New Labour colleagues still called 'the awkward squad'[39]), Miliband initiated a revision of the rules for leadership elections precisely to diminish the influence of the union vote.

The new system of one member one vote, oriented to encouraging a US primary-style vote for leadership candidates nominated from within the PLP, was initially opposed by the left. Yet the unintended consequence of this rule change opened the door for the move from protest to politics in Britain to take the form of almost 200,000 new members and 100,000 more 'supporters' signing up to elect Corbyn, beginning the process of making the Labour Party, with over 550,000 members today, the largest in Europe.

Of course, this did not happen spontaneously. It was in good part due to the actual momentum generated by Momentum. The emergence at the time of the Occupy movement of 'a cheeky and assertive digital Bennite social media project' called 'Red Labour' by an internet-savvy new generation of activists presaged the creation during the 2015 leadership election campaign, under the leadership of Jon Lansman, of Momentum as a new organization focused on mobilizing new members and supporters behind (and indeed in front of) Corbyn. With a data base that became its primary asset, Momentum activists not only played a crucial role in getting Corbyn elected as leader, but also re-elected again a year later in the face of the revolt supported by most Labour MPs. Even while soon surpassing the CLPD's earlier successes in mobilizing the majority of constituency delegates to vote for the left's resolutions at the annual party conference, the energy and creativity of Momentum's young activists was especially evident in organizing 'The World Transformed' as a parallel event of radical art and discussion which sharply contrasted with the trade show atmosphere under New Labour.

Perhaps the most significant aspect of the June 2017 election, very much more due to Momentum's strategic electoral activity both on the ground in canvassing as well as through the internet, was the greatly increased turnout by young people to vote Labour. This was achieved despite almost two years of constant denigration of Corbyn by many of his own MPs being amplified across the whole spectrum of the mainstream media, as well as against the drag of a central party machine more concerned with vetting than welcoming new members. With the greatest electoral support coming not only from students but also from working-class voters under 35, especially from the semi-skilled, unskilled and unemployed workers among them, this suddenly gave the Labour electorate a remarkably young cast, with a potentially very important shift in the party's class base.

The last time anything like this happened was a half century before, in the two elections of the mid-1960s, when a new generation of working-class voters belied the widespread notion that class political differentiation was a thing of the past by voting Labour in such large numbers. It was only after the profoundly disappointing experience of a Labour government desperately attempting to manage the growing contradictions of the British 'mixed economy' and its 'special relationship' with the American empire that a great many of the young working-class voters turned away from the Labour Party by the time of the 1970 election.

Labour's remarkable electoral success in 2017, especially among young working-class people, was based on the common revulsion against austerity among both private and public sector workers. This stands in sharp contrast to the former's impatience with, if not hostility to, the latter's strikes against the austerity policies of the Labour government during the 'winter of discontent' just before the election of Thatcher. The much more sympathetic attitude to the plight of public employees today was powerfully captured by the positive reception to Momentum's satirical campaign video (visited by no less than a third of all Facebook users in Britain) which – after featuring a home care worker, a firefighter and a policeman on the job turning to the camera to say 'I am paid too much'

74

– ends with a man in a pinstriped suit and bowler hat turning to the camera just before entering his London mansion to say 'I am not paid enough'.

Yet the Corbyn's team 'seemed unsure of what to do with its new recruits' beyond the 'highly impressive get-out-the-vote operation', as Tom Blackburn, a leading Momentum activist in the classically industrial city of Salford, pointed out in an especially insightful article in *New Socialist* immediately after the election. Noting that 'the Corbynite base as a whole remains somewhat inexperienced' – especially in terms of their ability 'to actively cultivate popular support for a radical political alternative, rather than assuming that there is sufficient support already latent, just waiting to be tapped into' – Blackburn argued that 'the leadership must now start to provide its rank and file supporters with clear guidance and encouragement if this project is to progress further.' What this especially required was 'clarity and honesty about the scale of the task facing Labour's new left, and the nature of that task as well – to re-establish the Labour Party as a campaigning force in working-class communities, to democratise its policymaking structures and to bring through the next generation of Labour left cadres, candidates and activists.'

In this respect, the priority now needed to shift to transforming Labour into the kind of party oriented to accomplishing this, especially since 'an unsupportive bureaucracy could simply withhold the resources and logistical support necessary to make radical community organising a reality nationwide. Members looking to open up local parties and experiment with new methods of organising can currently expect little support from an unreformed Labour HQ.' None of this was to suggest that

> the rank-and-file Labour left should just sit around and wait for help from on high before organising in their communities. Indeed, there is already a great deal of highly useful and relevant experience of grassroots organising among Labour members – the hands-on experience of anti-cuts campaigners and trade union activists is already substantial. Rank-and-file initiative can make substantial achievements. But for this sort of approach to solidly take hold nationwide, an attentive and supportive central party apparatus will be invaluable.[40]

The election of Momentum candidates as constituency and youth representatives to the party's National Executive Committee, and the NEC's appointment of one of the new generation of left trade union staff as the new General Secretary, may augur well for this (although the manner of the latter's selection by prior agreement between the party and union leader's offices does not). So does the establishment at party headquarters of a new 'community organising unit' to work with constituency Labour parties and trade unions to build alliances and campaign on key local issues. For its part, Momentum's tactical caution to avoid being drawn into a media-fuelled hysteria over the 'reselection' of all sitting MPs, as had been the case with CLPD's reform effort in the 1970s, did not divert it from winning support among party branches and conference delegates for concrete proposals for 'a democratic selection process for the 21st century', nor from getting many Momentum-backed candidates nominated at the parliamentary as well as the municipal council level.

Still, especially in relation to the intra-party Democracy Review[41] that has been set up by the NEC, the fundamental changes Max Shanly called for in the youth wing of the party will apply even more decisively to the party as a whole: 'The role of political education is to end one's alienation from ideas – and alongside recruitment and retention, our task must be to build the political and organisational quality of our party's youth in order to both understand and resist capitalism.' Yet in the party as a whole 'political education – the very bread and butter of the socialist movement – has been put on the backburner; when our members are taught, they are taught to follow, not to lead'. Changing this would have to go right down to the level of constituency parties in order to remould then into 'hubs of ongoing discussion, education and culture'.[42]

This needs to be taken even further. To credibly stress the possibilities rather than the limits of changing the Labour Party requires posing a fundamental challenge to the way the party has traditionally been rooted in the working class via the trade unions. Indeed, what needs to be remembered in this new conjuncture is that the defeat of the last socialist attempt to transform the Labour Party, in which young people like Jeremy Corbyn and Jon Lansman first cut their teeth, is that it was the left-wing union leadership who, having supported it through their block vote at party conference, pulled the plug on it in face of the inevitable divisions it created inside the labour movement.[43] The traditional relationship between the unions and the party reproduced a division of labour which proved incapable of nourishing and renewing working-class formation and the development of democratic capacities. In this context, the support Corbyn has so far secured from much of the union leadership needs to be turned into a challenge to the left union leadership to validate their role in the current attempt to change the Labour Party by changing their own organizations, not least through explicit socialist cadre development among their memberships.

In the face of the Labour Party's constitutional structures and parliamentarist orientations, let alone the powerful forces which still sustain New Labour's expression of contemporary capitalist dynamics, the struggle inside the party was always bound to be long and bitter, and its outcome very uncertain, even after important victories for the left in intra-party procedures and leadership selection. Indeed, it is to be expected that those determined to resist and reverse these gains, and more broadly to undermine socialist currents at the level of the leadership and the base, will always be prepared to ramp up their efforts and push them outwards as each new set of elections approaches in the hope that this will increase their leverage in the intra-party battle. Appreciating this, and learning how to counter it effectively, is one of the key reasons that political education at the base of the party, as well as the unions and the social movements is, however daunting and difficult, so crucial.

6

The state and the socialist challenge

Just a few years ago it would have seemed most unlikely that among those looking for the renewal of socialist possibilities in the twenty-first century it would be developments in the British Labour Party which would attract the most international attention. That this is the case today is a credit to the enthusiasm and creativity of a new generation of socialist activists in Britain and the political perseverance and dedication of a coterie of long-committed socialists around Jeremy Corbyn. Yet if the election of a Corbyn government in Britain is not to lead to heady euphoria quickly followed by profound disappointment on the left internationally, as was the case with Syriza in Greece, British realities need to be kept in sober perspective.

It is important to appreciate the very limited extent to which socialist commitment has, so far, actually taken shape as socialist strategy inside the Labour Party. At best it might be said that socialists in the leadership and at the base may be seen as engaged in trying to shift the balance of forces inside the party, and outside it in relation to the unions and social movements, and indeed even in Momentum, so as to bring the party to the point that a serious socialist strategy might be developed.

Labour's popular 2017 Election Manifesto, with its radical articulation of an economic programme 'for the many not the few', represents a conspicuous turn away from neoliberal austerity and the accommodation of New Labour governments to the Thatcherite legacy.[44] This is to be accomplished through progressive taxation measures, the enhancement of a broad array of public services as well as union and workers' rights, and the renationalization of railways and public utilities. It sets out an industrial strategy to create an 'economy that works for all' through the strategic use of public procurement and national and regional investment banks. Although much of this is cast as a 'new deal for business', oriented to making British industry more regionally balanced and internationally competitive, underpinned by what it calls a 'successful international financial industry', the emphasis clearly falls on state actions and changes to company law that would require finance and industry to make their activities more 'diverse' and 'socially useful' to meet the needs of workers, consumers and communities.

More telling regarding the socialist orientation of Corbyn's inner circle may be the *Alternative Models of Ownership* report, commissioned by John McDonnell, and released a few days before the election. Though not official party policy, the stress it put on the role of municipal public ownership and procurement policies to seed and nurture worker and community co-operatives was designed to encourage broad discussion of new socialist strategies. Also revived was the concern, always voiced by the Labour left since the nationalizations of the 1945 government, to avoid the replication of top-down corporate management in publicly owned enterprises by encouraging new forms of industrial democracy as well as accountability to 'diverse publics'.[45]

This clearly falls well short of representing a strategy for achieving a transition to socialism, whether as conceived in the old Clause IV commitment to 'the common ownership of the means of production, distribution and exchange and the best obtainable system of popular administration and control of each industry or service'; or, as it was later more vaguely put on the Labour left, taking over 'the commanding heights of the economy'. No less important, proposals for the expansion of co-ops and workers control at the enterprise level, while legitimately raising the *potential* transformative contribution of workers' collective knowledge, underplay how far workers' *actual* capacities have been constricted under capitalism. Moreover, the emphasis on decentralized forms of common ownership usually skirts the crucial question of how to integrate and coordinate enterprises, sectors and regions through democratic economic planning processes which are so necessary to avoid reproducing the types of particularistic and dysfunctional competitive market behaviour that socialists want to transcend.[46]

What is perhaps most problematic is the glaring silence on how the promotion of a high-tech, internationally competitive industrial strategy relates to the development of a transformational strategy to socialism.[47] And related to this, there are real strategic costs associated with the understandable reluctance to publically broach

the vexing question of how and when to introduce capital controls, so essential to investment
planning as well as to counter the blackmail of
governments via capital flight in open financial
markets. In contrast with the new left insurgency
of the 1970s, there is a marked avoidance today
of openly discussing the question of the need
to turn the whole financial system into a public
utility. In the absence of this, effective socialist
economic and social restructuring of Britain,
let alone with decentralization of significant
democratic decisions to the local community
level, cannot be realized.

This is not to say that merely calling for
sweeping immediate nationalizations really
addresses the strategic problems this entails.
As Tony Benn told the 1979 Labour Party
conference in speaking for the NEC against
adopting Militant's 'resolutionary' posture of
demanding the immediate nationalization of
the top 200 industrial and financial corporations,
simply failed to take seriously what it meant to
be 'a party of democratic, socialist reform'. While
averring he was a 'Clause IV socialist, becoming
more so as the years go by', Benn nevertheless
rightly insisted that any serious socialist strategy
had to begin from 'the usual problems of the

reformer: we have to run the economic system to protect our people who are locked into it while we change the system'.[48]

This stark dilemma was also seriously addressed by Seumas Milne (the former Guardian journalist who is today Corbyn's right-hand man) in his 1989 co-authored book, *Beyond the Casino Economy*. On the one hand, it argued that 'one of the necessary conditions for a socialist society would be to turn [the top] few hundred corporations into democratically owned and accountable public bodies'. On the other, it conceded that 'in the foreseeable circumstances of the next few years, the socialization of all large-scale private enterprise seems highly unlikely'; this limited 'what can plausibly be proposed as part of a feasible programme for a Labour government in the coming years – even one elected in an atmosphere of radical expectations'.[49]

The crucial point here is not to stubbornly insist on an immediate radicalization of policy that can only represent ineffective sloganeering. The constraints of the internal balance of forces in the party, as well as electoral ones, still shaped the Labour Manifesto. The measure of the Corbyn leadership in this regard should not be how explicitly socialist its policies are, but rather the extent to which it problematizes how to implement reform measures in such ways as to advance, rather than close off, future socialist possibilities. That is, to enhance – through the development of class, party and state capacities – the possibility of realizing socialist goals.

Here is where the lessons to be learned from the Syriza experience become especially important. One of its original leading cadre, Andreas Karitzis, who remained in the party apparatus while others rushed into the state, has recently articulated this extremely well in arguing that 'implementation procedures are the material foundations of a party's political strategy.' The advancement of policy goals without consideration of the specific changes that would need to take place in the relevant state apparatuses to actually implement those policies was bound to fail insofar as they did not recognize that decision-making processes at the parliamentary and governmental levels 'are just the peak of the iceberg of state policy. Implementing procedures are the mass of the iceberg below the water, i.e. the bulk of state policy ... there is no possibility that broad political decisions can actually shift state policy, whether through inadvertence or indifference to "how and who" will implement these decisions'[50]

The question of 'how' was disregarded in the

party debates over policy before Syriza's election to government 'either because of the inability to offer an answer or because it was seen as irrelevant in the face of internal party rivalry'. The result of this was that 'the dozens of committees that had been formed reproduced vague political confrontations instead of outlining specific implementation plans by sector to overcome obstacles and restructure state functions and institutions with a democratic orientation'. Above all,

> at the highest political organs, disagreements over the recommended political decision (about the current banks, debt, and so on) were tediously repeated as if SYRIZA had the ability to implement them … [This] pattern of political behaviour that proved particularly problematic … The end result was that the party did not focus on its basic duty: developing plans of action to address the difficult 'how?' of a different policy in the framework of an asphyxiated political environment. The obsessive adherence to lists of demands that are not attached to plans of action, and the acceptance of difficulties as a reason for adopting a more conventional governance mindset, did not advance the party's operational capability, and did not serve its political strategy.[51]

This strategic failure also proved critically important in relation to the lack of attention (as much or more by those who argued for 'Plan B') to drawing on the knowledges and practices of those at the base of the party in closest touch with the social movements so as to enhance the capacities of those who enter the state to try to change it. Strategic planning to this end must, as Karitzis puts it, 'not only involve the government, but requires methods of social and political mobilization at multiple levels and of a different nature than movements of social resistance and actions for attaining government power'. The potential for a more productive relationship was there, insofar as so many party members at the base were closely involved with the solidarity networks and other community-based initiatives, which initially became

the spark for acknowledging members' skills (formal education, technical expertise, work experience, etc.) and highlighting these abilities and qualifications as important elements for party work as well as facilitating the creative and productive inclusion of people outside its membership. Nonetheless, SYRIZA, as a collective political body was unable to utilise this enormous skill pool to expand and support its political strategy, because it did not develop the appropriate organisational receptors and 'extraction methods' for harnessing human potential.[52]

Perhaps the most unfortunate result of this was that grassroots participation exhausted itself 'in protest or support demonstrations, rather than in substantive and productive engagement'. Party local and regional branches 'formulated their own activity in the solidarity sector without using the, structure, network, infrastructure, and technical expertise of the Solidarity For All initiative or the party's central mechanism.'[53]

In terms of the lessons the Labour Party under Corbyn's leadership can draw from this, especially in light of Karitzis's argument here that 'effective methods of communication using new technologies in multiple ways' could have sustained 'a well-coordinated interface', it might especially have been hoped that the Labour's recent *Digital Democracy Manifesto* might have pointed in that direction. Unfortunately, it betrayed 'a rather narrow image of technology that concentrates on the internet, end-users and "networked individuals"… an image of publicness in the form of networks that nevertheless has security and privacy at its heart', as Nina Power has noted. The result is that the report contributes very little to how 'the new digital technologies help us to think about democratic economic planning', as Power goes on to do for the care services sector of the economy.[54]

This needs to be extended to thinking through the role of digital technology in the economic planning needed to turn the *Alternative Models of Ownership* report into a socialist strategy. Still more ambitiously, it should be applied to thinking through how to develop the planning capacities to transform financial services, Britain's dominant economic sector, into a public utility (starting with those banks rescued in the wake of the 2007-8 crisis that remain in public hands but are bizarrely still required to operate as competitive commercial enterprises).

To stress the importance of a democratic socialist strategy for entering the state through elections to the end of transforming the state is today less than ever a matter of discovering a smooth gradual road to socialism. Reversals, of various intensities, are inescapable. Governments reaching beyond capitalism will never have the luxury of 'circumstances they choose for themselves'.[55] Moreover, the basic problem for any government oriented to pursuing a socialist project is that the very challenge to capital's hegemony will likely spark, or aggravate, an economic crisis which will make it difficult to satisfy popular expectations for the promised relief from inequality and austerity. How to cope with this while not pushing off to an indefinite future the measures needed to begin the transformation of the state is the crucial socialist political challenge.

It is this tension among the various new state responsibilities which makes the role of socialist parties that will bring such governments to office so fundamental. Given the legitimacy and resources that inevitably will accrue to those party leaders who form the government, the autonomy of the party, which must more than ever keep its feet in the movements, is necessary in order to counter the pull from inside the state towards social democratization. This is why strategic preparations undertaken well before entering the state on how to avoid replicating the experience with social democracy are so very important. But even with this, the process of transforming the state cannot help but be complex, uncertain, crisis-ridden, with repeated interruptions.

Transformations of state apparatuses at local

or regional levels where circumstances and the balance of forces are more favourable may still be pursued, including developing alternative means of producing and distributing food, health care and other necessities at community levels. This could have the further benefit of facilitating and encouraging the involvement of women in local and party organisations, as well as stimulate autonomous movements moving in these directions through takeovers of land, idle buildings, threatened factories and transportation networks. All this may in turn spur developments at the higher levels of state power, ranging over time from codifying new collective property rights to developing and coordinating agencies of democratic planning. At some points in this process more or less dramatic initiatives of nationalization and socialization of industry and finance would have to take place, being careful to 'mind the gap' between participatory socialist politics and previous versions of state ownership.

Given how state apparatuses are now structured so as to reproduce capitalist social relations, their institutional modalities would need to undergo fundamental transformations so as to be able to implement all this. Public employees would themselves need to become explicit agents of transformation, aided and sustained in this respect by their unions and the broader labour movement. Rather than expressing defensive particularism, unions themselves would need to be changed fundamentally so as to actively engage in developing state workers' transformational capacities, including by establishing councils that link them to the recipients of state services.

Of course, the possibility of such state transformations will not be determined by what happens in one country alone. During the era of neoliberalism state apparatuses have become deeply intertwined with international institutions, treaties and regulations to manage and reproduce global capitalism. This has nothing at all to do with capital bypassing the nation state and coming to rely on a transnational state. Both the nature of the current crisis and the responses to it prove once again how much states still matter. Even in the most elaborate transnational institutional formation, the European Union, the centre of political gravity lies not in the supranational state apparatus headquartered in Brussels. It is, rather, the asymmetric economic and political power relations among the states of Europe that really determines what the EU is and does.

Any project for democratization at an international scale, such as those being advanced for the EU by many on the left in the wake of the Syriza experience, still depends on the balance of class forces and the particular institutional structures within each nation state. Changes in international institutions are contingent on transformations at the level of nation states. What above all needs to be born in mind amidst the continuing confusions and manoeuvrings around Brexit is the question of whether the Treaty of Rome let alone the provisions of Economic and Monetary Union always hindered rather than helped in projects for socialist transformation that could only be undertaken, even if not finally accomplished, within each state. The changes in international state apparatuses that should be pursued by socialists are those that would allow them more room for manoeuvre within each state. What socialist internationalism must mean today is an orientation to shifting the balances of forces in other countries and in international bodies so as to create more space for transformative forces in every country. This was one of the key lessons of 1917, and it is all the more true a century later.

The broad point here is that reform versus revolution is not a useful way to frame the dilemmas that socialists must today actually confront. Political hopes are inseparable from notions of what is possible, while possibility is itself intimately related to the role of socialist parties in working-class formation and reformation of the broadest possible kind. If a socialist project is, however, not to be stymied by the inherited state apparatuses, decisive focus on developing the agency and capacity for state transformation will be required. In this respect, socialist parties in the twenty-first century cannot see themselves as a kind of omnipotent *deus ex machina*. Precisely in order not to draw back from the 'prodigious scope of their own aims', as Marx once put it, they must 'engage in perpetual self-criticism' and deride 'the inadequacies, weak points and pitiful aspects of their first attempts'.[56]

NOTES

1   As *The Communist Manifesto* put it, in elaborating on the bourgeoisie's 'highly revolutionary role' historically; 'the bourgeoisie cannot exist without constantly revolutionizing the instruments of production, and thereby relations of production, and with them the whole relations of society... In a phrase, it creates a world in its own image'. Karl Marx, *Later Political Writings*, edited and translated by Terrell Carver, Cambridge, UK: Cambridge University Press, 1996, pp. 3-5. For a discussion of the continuing implications of this, see Leo Panitch, 'Capitalism, Socialism and Revolution', in Ralph Miliband, Leo Panitch, and John Saville, eds., *The Socialist Register 1989*, London: Merlin Press, 1989; and *Renewing Socialism: Transforming Democracy, Strategy and Imagination*, London: Merlin Press, 2009.

2   Between the 1987 American stock market crash and the investment banking collapse two decades later, there were upwards of a hundred distinct currency and banking crises as a direct outcome of global capital mobility. States were no longer in the business of 'crisis prevention' through regulations that might impede the free flow of capital; rather they were in the business of 'crisis containment', as the US Treasury itself put it in explaining why its central role had become 'firefighting'. See Leo Panitch and Sam Gindin, *The Making of Global Capitalism: The Political Economy of American Empire*, London: Verso, 2012, Chapters 10-12.

3   Perry Anderson, 'Renewals', *New Left Review*, 1(January/ February), 2000, pp. 7, 13. 'Whatever limitations persist to its practice, neo-liberalism as a set of principles rules undivided across the globe: the most successful ideology in world history'.

4   Andrew Murray, 'Jeremy Corbyn and the Battle for Socialism', *Jacobin*, 7 February 2016.

5   Marx, *Later Political Writings*, pp. 9-10.

6   See E.P. Thompson, *The Making of the English Working Class*, New York: Pantheon, 1964, pp. 9-11; and 'Eighteenth Century English Society: Class Struggle Without Class', *Social History*, 3(2), May 1978, pp. 133-65.

7   E. H. Hobsbawm, 'The Making of the Working Class, 1870-1914', *Uncommon People: Resistance, Rebellion and Jazz*, New York: The New Press, 1999, pp. 58-9. See also Geoff Eley, *Forging Democracy: The History of the Left in Europe, 1850-2000*, New York: OUP, 2002.

8   Robert Michels, *Political Parties: A Sociological Study of the Oligarchical Tendencies of Modern Democracy*, New York: Free Press, 1962.

9   Rosa Luxemburg, 'The Russian Revolution', in Peter Hudis and Kevin Anderson, eds., *The Rosa Luxemburg Reader,* New York: Monthly Review Press, 2004, pp. 304-6.

10 Isaac Deutscher, *The Prophet Armed*, London: OUP, 1954, pp. 505-6.

11 Quoted in L. Panitch and S. Gindin, 'Moscow, Togliatti, Yaroslavl: Perspectives on Perestroika' in Dan Benedict et al., eds., *Canadians Look at Soviet Auto Workers' Unions*, Toronto: CAW, 1992, p. 19.

12 'An American Proposal', *Fortune*, May 1942. See L. Panitch & S. Gindin, 2012, pp. 67-8.

13 See Leo Panitch, 'Socialist Renewal and the Labour Party', *Socialist Register* 1988, pp. 319-65; and Leo Panitch and Colin Leys, *The End of Parliamentary Socialism: from New Left to New Labour*, Verso: 2001.

14 André Gorz, 'Reform and Revolution', in Ralph Miliband and John Saville, eds., *The Socialist Register 1968*, London: Merlin Press, 1968; Lucio Magri, 'Problems of the Marxist Theory of the Revolutionary Party', *New Left Review*, 60 (March/April), 1970; Tony Benn, *The New Politics: A Socialist Reconnaissance*, Fabian Tract 402, September 1970; Ralph Miliband, 'Moving On', in Ralph

Miliband and John Saville, eds., *The Socialist Register 1976*, London: Merlin Press, 1976; Ralph Miliband, *Marxism and Politics*, Oxford: OUP, 1977; Sheila Rowbotham, Lynne Segal, and Hilary Wainwright, *Beyond the Fragments: Feminism and the making of Socialism*, London: Merlin, 1979.

15   Nicos Poulantzas, 'Towards a Democratic Socialism', *State, Power, Socialism,* London: NLB, 1978. The quotes below are drawn from pp. 256-261.

16   Gorz, 'Reform and Revolution', p. 112.

17   Gorz, 'Reform and Revolution', pp. 132-3. Lucio Magri ('Problems of the Marxist Theory of the Revolutionary Party", p. 128) similarly called for new workers councils 'right across society (factories, offices, schools), with their own structures as mediating organizations between party, union, and state institutions, for which all of the latter needed to act as elements of stimulus and synthesis'. And even though he presented this in terms of the 'need for a creative revival of the theme of *soviets* [as] essential to resolve the theoretical and strategic problems of the Western Revolution', this was directed at offsetting the total dominance of the party, and emphatically did not mean re-endorsing a dual power strategy for 'smashing the state'.

18   Poulantzas, 'Towards a Democratic Socialism', pp. 256, 258.

19   Ralph Miliband, *Class Power and State Power*, London: Verso, 1983, esp. Chapters 2-4.

20   Goran Therborn, *What Does the Ruling Class Do When it Rules? State Apparatuses and State Power under Feudalism, Capitalism and Socialism*, NLB: London, 1978, pp. 279-80.

21   See however Greg Albo, David Langille and Leo Panitch eds., *A Different Kind of State: Popular Power and Democratic Administration*, Toronto: OUP, 1993.

22   See Sam Gindin, 'Chasing Utopia', *Jacobin*, 10 March 2016.

23   Poulantzas, 'Towards a Democratic Socialism', p. 262.
24   Bernie Sanders, 'Prepared Remarks: The Political Revolution Continues', 16 June, 2016. https://berniesanders.com/political-revolution-continues.
25   Dan La Botz, 'Life After Bernie: People's Summit Searches for the Movement's Political Future', *New Politics,* 21 June 2016. http://newpol.org.
26   See Steve Williams and Rishi Awatramani, 'New Working-Class Organizations and the Social Movement Left'; and Mark Dudzic and Adolph Reed, Jr., 'The Crisis of Labour and the Left in the United States', both in Leo Panitch and Greg Albo, eds., *Socialist Register 2015: Transforming Classes,* London: Merlin Press, 2014.
27   See Costas Eleftheriou, 'The Uneasy 'Symbiosis': Factionalism and Radical Politics in Synaspismos', paper prepared for 4th Hellenic Observatory PhD Symposium, n.d.
28   Michalis Spourdalakis, 'Left Strategy in the Greek Cauldron: Explaining Syriza's Success', in Leo Panitch, Greg Albo, and Vivek Chibber, eds., *Socialist Register 2013: The Question of Strategy,* London: Merlin Press, 2012, p. 102.
29   Available at: https://left.gr/news/political-resolution-1st-congress-SYRIZA.
30   'Syriza and Socialist Strategy', *International Socialism,* No. 146, April 2015 (transcript of a debate between Alec Callinicos and Stathis Kouvelakis, London, 25 February 2015).
31   Costas Douzinas, 'The Left in Power? Notes on Syriza's Rise, Fall and (Possible) Second Rise', *Near Futures Online,* March 2016. Available at: http://nearfuturesonline.org.
32   Michalis Spourdalakis, 'Becoming Syriza Again', *Jacobin,* 31 January 2016.
33   See www.solidarity4all.gr/; https://www.greenleft.org.au/content/greece-solidarity-action-visit-solidarity4all-clinic.

34 Ralph Miliband, 'Moving On', in Ralph Miliband and John Saville, eds, *The Socialist Register 1976*, London: Merlin, 1976, pp. 128, 138.

35 See Andrew Murray's sharp critique of the Left Unity initiative, 'Left Unity or Class Unity? Working-class politics in Britain', in Leo Panitch, Greg Albo and Vivek Chibber, *Registering Class: Socialist Register 2014*, London: Merlin, 2013. Murray himself could hardly have imagined then that only three years later he would be seconded from his position as chief of staff of Unite, Britain largest union, to the Labour party leader's election campaign office.

36 Tony Benn, 'Democratic Politics,' Fabian Autumn Lecture, 3 November 1971, in *Speeches by Tony Benn*, pp. 277-9; Tony Benn, *A New Politics: A Socialist Reconnaissance*, Fabian Tract 402, September 1970, p. 9; see also 'Tony Benn: Articulating a New Socialist Politics', Panitch and Leys, *The End of Parliamentary Socialism*, pp. 50-1.

37 Alex Nunns, *The Candidate: Jeremy Corbyn's Improbable Path to Power*, London: Or Books, 2018, p. 147.

38 Richard Seymour, *Corbyn: The Strange Rebirth of Radical Politics*, London: Verso, 2017, p. 174.

39 Nunns, *The Candidate*, p. 147.

40 Tom Blackburn, 'Corbynism from Below', *New Socialist*, June 12, 2017. https://newsocialist.org.uk/corbynism-from-below/

41 https://labour.org.uk/about/democracy-review-2017/.

42 Max Shanly, 'Toward a New Model Young Labour' *The Bullet*, November 27, 2017. https://socialistproject.ca/2017/11/b1516/.

43 See Panitch and Leys, *The End of Parliamentary Socialism*, esp. chapter 8.

44 *For the Many, Not the Few*. https://labour.org.uk/manifesto/.

45   *Alternative Models of Ownership,* Report to the Shadow
     Chancellor of the Exchequer and Shadow Secretary
     of State for Business, Energy and Industrial Strategy.
     https://labour.org.uk/wp-content/uploads/2017/10/
     Alternative-Models-of-Ownership.pdf.
46   See Hilary Wainwright, *A New Politics from the Left,*
     Cambridge: Polity, 2018.
47   See Paul Mason, *Post-Capitalism*: London: Allen Lane,
     2015.
48   Quoted in Panitch and Leys, *The End of Parliamentary
     Socialism*, pp.174-5.
49   Nicholas Costello, Jonathan Michie and Seumas Milne,
     Beyond the Casino Economy, London: Verso, 1989, pp.
     254-5.
50   Andreas Karitzis, *The European Left in Times of Crises:
     Lessons from Greece,* Amsterdam: Transnational
     Institute, 2017, p. 29.
51   Ibid, pp. 30-32.
52   Ibid, pp. 20-21.
53   Ibid, pp. 23-4.
54   Nina Power, 'Digital Democracy', in L. Panitch and G.
     Albo eds., *Rethinking Democracy: Socialist Register
     2018,* London: Merlin, 2017, p. 174.
55   Marx, 'The Eighteenth Brumaire of Louis Bonaparte',
     Later Political Writings, p. 32.
56   Ibid., p. 35.

Also from The Merlin Press

Rethinking Democracy: Socialist Register 2018
Edited by Leo Panitch & Greg Albo

Have we now reached 'the end of history' with the triumph of capitalist liberal democracy? Is socialism an enemy of democracy? Or could socialism develop, expand and enhance democracy? The antagonism between liberalism and democratic processes is increasingly visible: we can see the contradictions of capitalist globalization, a rise of authoritarian politics in many states, and concepts of post-democracy, anti-politics, and the like gaining currency in theoretical and political debate.

This volume seeks a re-appraisal of actually-existing liberal democracy today, but its main goal is to help lay the foundations for new visions and practices in the development of socialist democracy. Amidst the contradictions of neoliberal capitalism today, the responsibility to sort out the relationship between socialism and democracy has never been greater. No revival of socialist politics in the 21st century can occur apart from founding new democratic institutions and practices.

978-0-85036-733-1 paperback £17.95
978-0-85036-732-4 hardback £60.00

www.merlinpress.co.uk